When it rains, puddles form on the ground.

As well as being fun to jump into, puddles can be a home, or a drink, for small animals and birds.

Frogs like this one need puddles and ponds to lay their eggs in.

This crow is having a drink from a puddle.

When a raindrop hits a puddle, it makes a little crown-shaped splash. Then a pattern of rings forms — each one bigger than the one before.

Splash!

How many rings can you see?

How quickly can you say this rhyme?

Doctor Foster went to Gloucester,
In a shower of rain.
He stepped in a puddle,
Right up to his middle,
And never went there again.

You might think that raindrops are droplet-shaped, but in fact they are not!

 Smaller raindrops (those less than 2mm across) are perfectly round.

Raindrops that are about 2mm across have flat bottoms.

 Bigger raindrops (between 2mm and 5mm across) are shaped like a bean.

Any raindrops that get bigger than 5mm across split into two smaller ones.

Size guide: 5mm ● 2mm ●

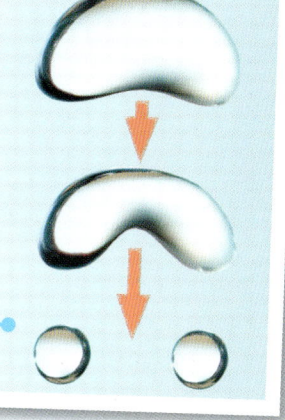

Where does rain come from?

1. The sun shines on the sea and heats it up.
2. Liquid from the sea evaporates (turns into little droplets, which float up into the sky).
3. The droplets condense (form clouds) in the sky.
4. The rain falls from the clouds.
5. The rain on the land forms rivers, which flow back down to the sea to be evaporated again.

All rain comes from clouds, but not all clouds make rain. Tall, dark, towering clouds with flat bottoms often bring storms or rain showers, but thin, wispy clouds hardly ever do.

Can you see the rain falling from this storm cloud?

Clouds like these are common on a dry summer's day. They do not bring rain.

When it is raining and sunny at the same time, the sunlight shines in the raindrops and a rainbow is made in the sky.

Look at the rainbow below. Going from the outside of the rainbow to the inside, the stripes are red, orange (/**o**rinj/), yellow, green, blue, indigo and violet (/**vie**ɛlɛt/).

- red
- orange
- yellow
- green
- blue
- indigo
- violet

Sometimes there is a double rainbow, with a bright rainbow underneath a slightly fainter one. When this happens, the stripes of the top rainbow go in the opposite order – from violet to red instead of red to violet!

Did you know that a rainbow is not arch-shaped? We can only see part of it from the ground. If you saw it from a plane in the sky, you would see a whole rainbow ring!

Different parts of the planet get different amounts of rain.

You will not be surprised to learn that rainforests get a lot of rain. The clue is in the name: rain-forest!

There is a thick mist in this forest.

Nor will it surprise you to learn that deserts like this one get very little rain.

This desert is very hot as well as very dry.

But it might surprise you to learn that the part of the planet that gets the least rain of all is Antarctica.

Antarctica has a lot of snow on the ground, but no rainfall.

Antarctica is a very cold desert that has snow instead of sand. The part of Antarctica with the lowest rainfall of all is called the Dry Valleys. There has been no rain there for a very long time.

Unlike Antarctica, the UK is well-known for its wet weather, so you might think that the wettest part of the planet is somewhere in Wales or Scotland, but in fact the north-east of India (/**In**deeɛ/) gets much more rain! In one year, one town in India had 14,234mm of rain, but the UK only gets about 1,154mm a year.

The whole of north-east India gets a lot of rain.

India has a monsoon rainy season, when it gets a lot of rain in a short time. A monsoon is a sea breeze that can bring a lot of rain. Monsoon rains happen when the land is much hotter than the sea.

Monsoons are common in the tropics. Brazil, West Africa, Myanmar and Bangladesh all have monsoons.

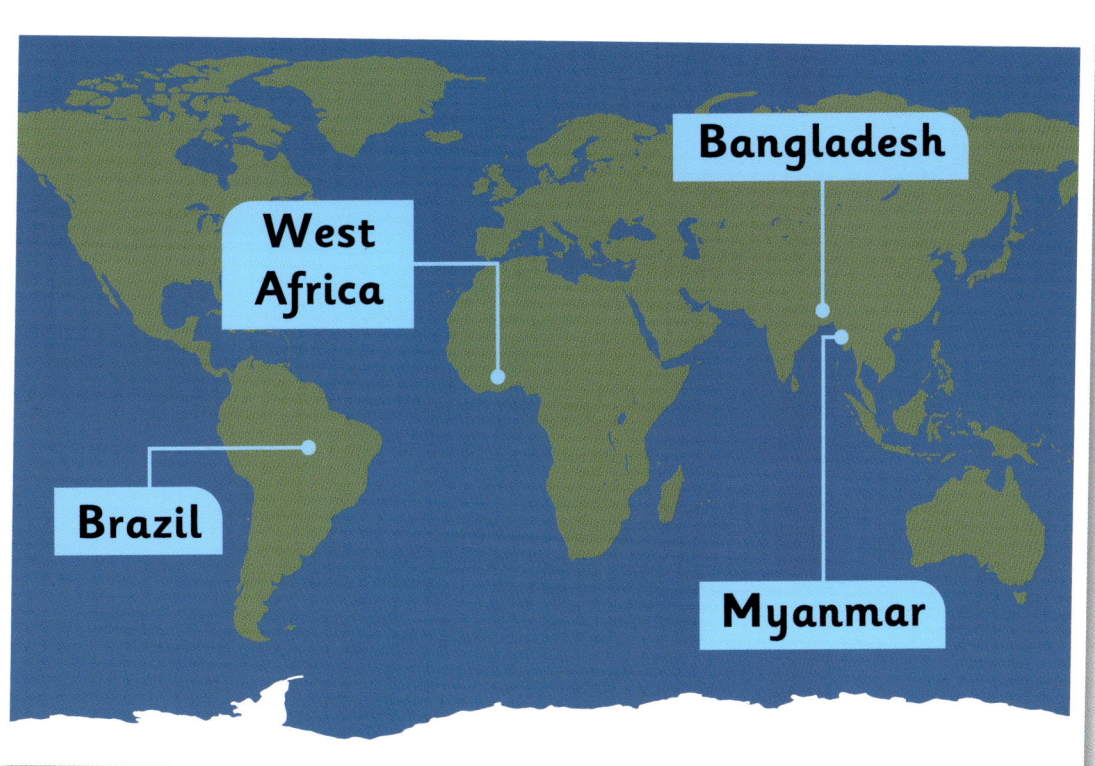

Monsoons can bring a dry season as well, when there is little or no rain. When there is no rain at all for many weeks, it is called a drought. In a drought, the ground can become so dry that it cracks.

dry, cracked soil

farmer

Droughts are very bad for farmers, because all food crops need some rain to grow. In this way, drought affects all of us because we all eat the food that farmers grow.

Some crops, such as rice (/ries/), can only grow when the ground is very wet.

This farmer is growing his crops in a paddy field (/**fee**ɘld/). Look how wet the soil is!

Different crops need different amounts of rain. Beans, melons, okra and peppers can all grow well without very much rain.

Which of these foods do you like best?

peppers

okra

melon

beans

We can see how much rain has fallen where we are by looking at a rain gauge (/gaij/). This is a tall, thin tube with ruler marks printed on the side.

As the rain falls, the tube fills up. You can see the amount of rainfall by reading the numbers on the side.

Rainfall is recorded in mm or inches.

This tube is empty, which tells us that there has been no rain lately.

You can make your own rain gauge from a ruler and an empty jar. The jar must have a flat bottom and straight sides.

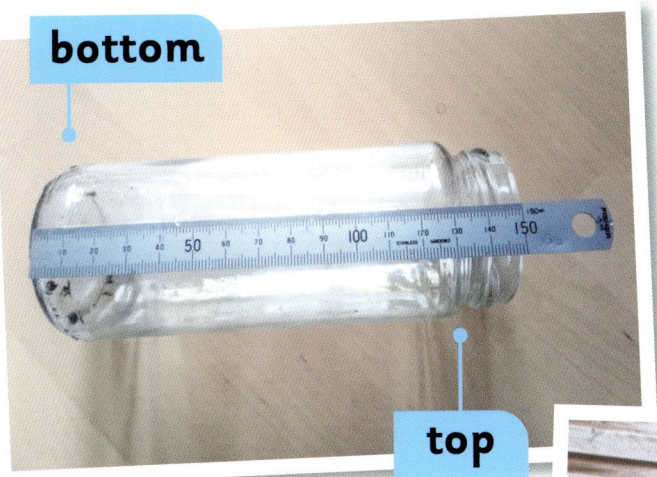

bottom

top

Tape your ruler to the side of the jar, with the numbers going from the bottom to the top.

Put it outside to see how much it rains where you are.

The jar must not be underneath anything, because this will stop the rain falling into it.

rain

When it is cold and raining outside, it is very important to keep yourself dry.

Put on a raincoat and rubber boots, or a rainproof outfit, and carry an umbrella.

Did you know that the smell of rain on dry soil has a name? It is called petrichor!